C000205072

Orders: Please contact How2Become Ltd, Suite 14, 50 Churchill Square Business Centre, Kings Hill, Kent ME19 4YU.

You can order through Amazon.co.uk under ISBN 9781910602898, via the website www.How2Become.com or through Gardners.com.

ISBN: 9781910602898

First published in 2016 by How2Become Ltd.

Typeset for How2Become Ltd by Anton Pshinka.

Disclaimer

Every effort has been made to ensure that the information contained within this guide is accurate at the time of publication. How2Become Ltd is not responsible for anyone failing any part of any selection process as a result of the information contained within this guide. How2Become Ltd and their authors cannot accept any responsibility for any errors or omissions within this guide, however caused. No responsibility for loss or damage occasioned by any person acting, or refraining from action, as a result of the material in this publication can be accepted by How2Become Ltd.

The information within this guide does not represent the views of any third party service or organisation.

GCSE Spanish Is Easy

www.How2Become.com

As part of this product you have also received FREE access to online tests that will help you to pass GCSE Spanish Is Easy

To gain access, simply go to:

www.PsychometricTestsOnline.co.uk

Get more products
for passing any test at:

www.how2become.com

CONTENTS

INTRODUCTION TO YOUR GUIDE

INTRODUCTION TO YOUR GUIDE

Hello, and welcome to your guide to GCSE Spanish. Written by How2Become the UK's leading career specialists, this book will provide you with everything you need to revise GSCE Spanish in as complete and concise a manner a possible.

GCSE Spanish is Easy will become your go-to guide for all the information and advice you need for studying and passing GCSE Spanish. Packed fu of grammar resources, vocabulary lists, sample questions, and top tips this revision guide will complement student's classroom learning and exam preparation.

GCSE Spanish Examination

GCSE Spanish is designed to test your understanding of the language as well as your ability to use it in a variety of situations. No matter which exam board your school uses, you will need to have a command of essential verbs and vocabulary, and be extremely comfortable with core elements of grammar. Of course, this will be done through the study of specific modules focusing on general topics such as 'the environment' or 'leisure activities In a nutshell, getting a good grade in GSCE Spanish will require an ability t respond to and express many ideas and opinions, with accuracy.

As you know, you will have a **reading** exam, a **listening** exam, and **speaking** exam, as well as controlled assessments to test your **writte communication** in Spanish.

So, being able to apply your knowledge of the module topics effectively, in variety of mediums and contexts, is crucial for securing a high grade.

What the syllabus says

Undoubtedly, it would be extremely helpful to be aware of what the aim of the GCSE Spanish course are. The government has set out specifi objectives to include in the syllabus, in order to ensure teachers and exam boards are assessing particular skills and knowledge required to obtain GCSE in Spanish.

By providing a detailed outline of the course, teachers and exam boards are able to tailor their resources to equip their students with basic Spanish knowledge, which will ultimately add context and a clearer focus to learning and revision.

Here are the key aims and outcomes of GSCE Spanish according to the syllabus:

- *To enable students to communicate accurately, confidently, coherently, spontaneously and independently in Spanish, with an enriched vocabulary in a fluent manner and variety of contexts;*

- *To enable students to understand clearly articulated Spanish in standard speech, at near-normal speed, and to develop their ability and ambition to communicate with native speakers;*

- *To develop students' ability to respond to a range of (appropriately adapted) authentic Spanish written material, including news articles and other literary texts;*

- *To encourage students to develop a wider awareness and understanding of Spanish culture, and see beyond the common clichés in relation to Spain.*

The exams

The four elements of your language course will be measured and calculated, and will then count towards your overall grade. Luckily, major exam boards, including AQA, Edexcel and OCR, all have a similar way of calculating the overall grade based on the four exams. In a full Spanish GCSE course from any of these exam boards, this is how you will be assessed:

Listening:

You will be played extracts of Spanish speech, which will be of varying speeds, lengths and difficulty, and will be both formal and informal.

The questions, presented in English, are designed to test your ability in identifying, understanding, and responding to information.

- Answers are in Spanish and English.

  (Examination result = 20% of your final grade)

Reading:

- You will be presented with text in a variety of forms (e.g. emails, newspapers brochures), which will be of increasing complexity.
- Questions are given in English and will test how well you identify understand, and respond to information.
- Answers are in Spanish and English.

  (Examination result = 20% of your final grade)

Speaking:

- You will carry out two tasks (e.g. debate/discussion) that require you t interact with another speaker, who will most likely be your teacher.
- You will be marked on your use of Spanish to present ideas and informatior in multiple contexts and settings.
- It will also be marked by your teacher.

  (Controlled Assessment result = 30% of your final grade)

Writing:

- You will carry out two writing tasks on different subjects, in exam condition at your school.
- You will be marked on your ability to convey ideas and points of view clearly, which are relevant to the task.

  (Controlled Assessment result = 30% of your final grade)

VITAL VOCABULARY

This chapter will deal with core vocabulary, phrases and verbs that are absolutely vital to understanding and communicating in Spanish at any level.

Strong knowledge of this content will provide an excellent foundation for all further study, so although you will probably already be comfortable with a lot of it, it can do no harm to remind yourself of the basics.

WORKING WITH NUMBERS

Being comfortable with numbers is vital at this level of Spanish study, as it is GUARANTEED that somewhere in an exam, your ability to understand and respond accurately using numbers will be tested. Examiners love to present numbers to you in the form of percentages, timetables or people's ages, but all they really want to do is check that you know them.

Luckily, as you know, it is often quite simple to form numbers in Spanish; there are just a few things to remember. Still, it can do no harm to refresh your memory, and be sure to look out for our TOP TIPS!

0-10

0	cero
1	uno
2	dos
3	tres
4	cuatro
5	cinco
6	seis
7	siete
8	ocho
9	nueve
10	diez

1-15

11	once
12	doce
13	trece
14	catorce
15	quince

TOP TIP!

Note that these numbers are words in their own right: not formed with combinations of smaller ones (as many are below).

6-19

16	dieciséis
17	diecisiete
18	dieciocho
19	diecinueve

TOP TIP!

These numbers are written as a shortened version of saying '10+6', '10+7' etc.

The preferred way of writing 'sixteen', for example, is now 'dieciséis', rather than 'diez y seis'. This is because writing these numbers out in full like this is becoming more and more old-fashioned.

(Note: the accent that is now required in 16!)

20-29

20	veinte
21	veintiuno
22	veintidós
23	veintitrés
24	veinticuatro
25	veinticinco
26	veintiséis
27	veintisiete
28	veintiocho
29	veintinueve

TOP TIP!

These numbers are written as a shortened version of saying '20+1', '20+2' etc.

Similarly, as above, the preferred way of writing 'twenty-one', for example, is now '*veintiuno*', rather than '*veinte y uno*'.

(Note: the accents that are now required with 22, 23 and 26!)

30-101

30	treinta
31	treinta y uno
32	treinta y dos
40	cuarenta
50	cincuenta
60	sesenta
70	setenta
80	ochenta
90	noventa
100	cien
101	ciento uno

TOP TIP!

Beyond 30, numbers are written out as 30+1, 30+2 etc.

(E.g. 'sixty-four' is '*sesenta y cuatro*')

Note:

Unlike some examples above, with numbers above thirty, always write them out in full in this way. (E.g. 'thirty-one' is always '*treinta y uno*', **never** '*treintiuno*')

However, note 101 is not written out as 100+1, rather '100 1'

(I.e. 'one hundred and one' is '*ciento uno*', **NOT** '*ciento y uno*')

TEST YOURSELF!

- Write 'fourteen' in Spanish: _____

- Write 'nineteen' in Spanish: _____

- Write 'veintiocho' in English: _____

- Write 'seventy-two' in Spanish: _____

- Write 'one hundred and one' in Spanish:

_____

200-900

200	doscientos
250	doscientos cincuenta
300	trescientos
400	cuatrocientos
500	quinientos
600	seiscientos
700	setecientos
800	ochocientos
900	novecientos

TOP TIP!

Note that when writing numbers in the hundreds, do not use 'y' between the first and second digits.

(I.e. 'four hundred and thirty' is 'cuatrocientos treinta', **NOT** 'cuatrocientos y treinta')

1000 +

1.000	mil
1.500	mil quinientos
2.000	dos mil
10.000	diez mil
10.500	diez mil quinientos
100.000	cien mil
150.000	ciento cincuenta mil
250.000	doscientos cincuenta mil
500.000	quinientos mil
1.000.000	un millón
2.000.000	dos millones
2.500.000	dos millones quinientos mil

TOP TIP!

Note how digits over three figures long are written in Spanish! Instead of a comma or no punctuation, a full stop is used.

Also, saying 'one million' in Spanish is very similar to that in English. Just be careful to change '*millón*' to '*millones*' when writing 'two million' or more! Make those plurals agree, and look where the accent disappears!

TEST YOURSELF!

- Write 'two hundred and fifty-nine' in Spanish:

  _____

- Write 'four hundred and twelve' in Spanish:

  _____

- Write '*diez mil ochocientos*' in English:

  _____

- Write 'two hundred and fifty thousand, seven hundred and ninety-three' in Spanish:

  _____

- Write '*dos millones seiscientos tres mil trescientos cincuenta y uno*' in English:

  _____

Common ways you'll have to deal with numbers

So, you've learnt what the numbers themselves are, but of course there ar
several ways that numbers are used in a language, which go beyond counting
You will need to be familiar with the common ways in which numbers manifes
themselves in everyday speech, so review this section diligently.

Putting things in order:

NUMBER	SPANISH SPELLING	SPANISH ABBREVIATION
First	primero	1º
Second	segundo	2º
Third	tercero	3º
Fourth	cuarto	4º
Fifth	quinto	5º
Sixth	sexto	6º
Seventh	séptimo	7º
Eighth	octavo	8º
Ninth	noveno	9º
Tenth	décimo	10º

The Spanish ordinal numbers listed before are correct when simply formin
a list, for example when saying the order in which sprinters finished in a race
However, agreements have to be made when they appear before nouns. C
course, these agreements are determined by the noun's gender, as well as
they are in the singular or plural.

For example:

Masculine noun (singular):   *El segundo año*   ⟶   The second year

Feminine noun (singular):   *La segunda vez*   ⟶   The second time

TOP TIP!

As stated above, these agreements are pretty simple to make, just look out for a couple of oddities when using the Spanish equivalents of 'first' and 'third' before a noun!

Unlike *'segundo'*, for example, to make 'first' agree with a singular masculine noun, it is simply *'primer'* – without an 'o' at the end. However, the singular feminine form is a more standard *'primera'*. Also, the plural masculine form is *'primeros'*. It is the same story with 'third': *'tercer'*, *'tercera'*, *'terceros'*, *'terceras'*.

TELLING THE TIME:

Of course, asking and telling the time is a very common use of numbers i everyday language. There is a strong possibility that you will have to interpr times or timetables in some way in your reading or listening exam. Althoug you will probably feel comfortable with this section already, make sure you'v learned it well enough to avoid any silly errors in the future!

It's one o'clock   ⟶   **Es la una**

It's two o'clock   ⟶   **Son las dos**

It's three o'clock   ⟶   **Son las tres**

It's four o'clock   ⟶   **Son las cuatro**

It's five o'clock   ⟶   **Son las cinco**

It's six o'clock   ⟶   **Son las seis**

(and so on...)

TOP TIP!

Note that one o'clock is the only time in the singular!

This is because the feminine articles; '*la*' and '*las*' refer to '*hora*' (meaning 'hour'), and there is only one hour that needs to be referred to for 1 o'clock!

TEST YOURSELF!

Write out the times shown on the clocks below, in Spanish.

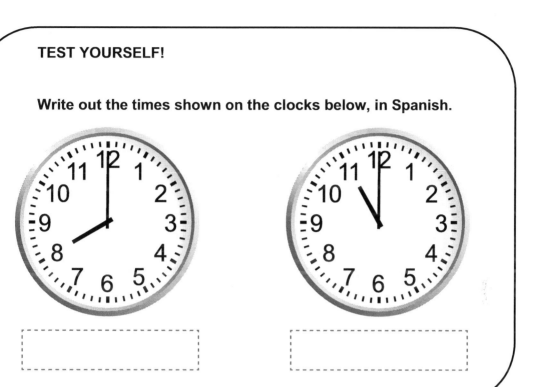

In Spanish, phrases like 'half past' and 'quarter to' are formed just as simply as they are in English. All you need to do is write the hour followed by 'y' or 'menos' plus the number of minutes past/before the hour you want to say! See below:

It's five past one	⟶	*Es la una y cinco*
It's ten past two	⟶	*Son las dos y diez*
It's quarter past three	⟶	*Son las tres y cuarto*
It's half past four	⟶	*Son las cuatro y media*
It's quarter to five	⟶	*Son las cinco menos cuarto*
It's ten to six	⟶	*Son las seis menos diez*
It's five to seven	⟶	*Son las siete menos cinco*

It's midday   →   ***Es mediodía***

It's midnight   →   ***Es medianoche***

TOP TIP!

Note that '*mediodía*' takes an 'o' in the middle, and '*medianoche*' takes an 'a'.

This is because '*día*' is a masculine word in its own right and '*noche*' is feminine!

To distinguish between a.m. and p.m. in Spanish, all you need to do is insert '*de la mañana*' (in the morning), '*de la tarde*' (in the afternoon) or '*de la noche*' (in the evening), after the time !

For example:

- **"It's 8am."**

"*Son las ocho de la mañana.*"

- **"What is the time?"**
- **"It's 2:30pm."**

"*¿Qué hora es?*"

"*Son las dos y media de la tarde*"

- **"Come to the studio at 9pm."**

"*Venga al estudio a las nueve de la noche.*"

TEST YOURSELF!

Write out the times shown on the clocks below, in Spanish.

TEST YOURSELF!

Write out the times shown on the clocks below, in Spanish. This time, to differentiate between a.m and p.m, include the expressions *'de la mañana', 'de la tarde'* and *'de la noche'!*

Times of day :

Sunrise	The early hours	The morning	Midday
La salida del sol	**La madrugada**	**La mañana**	**El mediodía**
The afternoon	The evening/night	Sunset	Late at night
La tarde	**La noche**	**La puesta del sol**	**A altas horas de la noche**

Fill in the boxes!

El búho prefiere...

El gallo canta en...

PRACTICE EXAM QUESTION

My timetable

Three British students describe their school timetables. Read the conversation and then answer the questions below, **in English**.

Rachel: En mi caso, yo necesito llegar al colegio a las nueve de la mañana para estar allí cuando pasan lista. Después, voy a mi clase de español que termina a las diez y cuarto. Mi siguiente clase termina a las once de la mañana.

Mo: En mi colegio, las clases empiezan a las ocho y media de la mañana, con un descanso para comer a la una y veinte. Mis compañeros y yo pasamos el resto de la tarde estudiando. Podemos volver a casa a las cuatro menos veinte de la tarde.

Josie: Mi asignatura favorita es la informática. Es mi primera clase del día, a las ocho menos cinco. Así que salgo de casa a las siete de la mañana para llegar a tiempo porque es una clase importante para mí.

Question 1

At what time does Rachel have to get to school?

Question 2

What time does Mo's school break for lunch?

Question 3

What time does Josie's first lesson start?

Question 4

Who gets to go home at 3:40pm?

Question 5

Who leaves the house at 7am?

Question 6

Whose lunch break starts at 1:20pm?

(Answers are provided at the end of the book).

CALENDARS AND DATES

Although you are probably familiar with the days of the week and the months it is all but guaranteed that you will have to deal with them in an exam situation So, it can do no harm to refresh your memory of this vocabulary.

Watch out for our TOP TIPS!

Days of the week:

lunes	martes	miércoles	jueves	viernes	sábado	doming
Monday	**Tuesday**	**Wednesday**	**Thursday**	**Friday**	**Saturday**	**Sunda**

> ### TOP TIP!
> Note that unlike the English language, the days of the week do not capitalise the first letter in Spanish – unless they are at the start of a sentence, of course!

El fin de semana	⟶	*The weekend*
El lunes pasado	⟶	*Last Monday*
El próximo martes	⟶	*Next Tuesday*
Los miércoles	⟶	*On Wednesdays*
Cada jueves **Todos los jueves**	⟶	*Each/Every Thursday*

Key phrases:

Hoy	Today
Ayer	Yesterday
Mañana	Tomorrow
El día siguiente	The following day
Dentro de una semana/ En una semana	In a week's time
Hace una semana	A week ago

TEST YOURSELF!

Translate the following sentences:

- 'Los viernes practico kárate en el polideportivo.'

  _____

- 'Ayer visité el Museo Guggenheim por primera vez.'

  _____

- 'Trabajo como voluntario cada semana en la ciudad.'

  _____

- 'My friend lost his phone last month.'

  _____

- 'Today is Sunday, and I am going to cook a big breakfast like I do every week.'

  _____

Months of the year:

As you know, the vast majority of these are very similar to their English equivalents, just be aware of the odd one out! Also, as with the days of the week, do not capitalise the first letter of the months of the year.

enero	**febrero**	**marzo**	**abril**
January	*February*	*March*	*April*

mayo	**junio**	**julio**	**agosto**
May	*June*	*July*	*August*

septiembre	**octubre**	**noviembre**	**diciembre**
September	*October*	*November*	*December*

Spanish National Holidays:

El 1 de enero – Día de Año Nuevo	*New Year's Day*
El 6 de enero – Día de los Reyes Magos	*Three Kings' Day or Epiphany – Hispanic celebration in honour of the Three Wise Men*
El viernes anterior al Domingo de Ramos – Viernes Santo	*The last Friday before Easter – Good Friday*
Lunes de Pascua	*Easter Monday*
El 1 de mayo – Día del Trabajador	*Labour Day*
El 12 de octubre – Fiesta Nacional de España	*National Day – Commemorating Christopher Columbus' discovery of the Americas*
El 6 de diciembre – Día de la Constitución	*Constitution Day – Commemorating the day in 1978 in which the Spanish chose their current constitution.*
El 25 de diciembre – Navidad	*Christmas Day*

¿Cuál es la fecha de hoy?, ¿Qué día es hoy? – *What is the date today?*

Hoy es el 21 de abril – *Today is the 21st of April.*

TOP TIP!

Make sure you are familiar with these key phrases:

Este mes – *This month*

El mes pasado – *Last month*

El próximo mes – *Next month*

A principios del mes/A primeros de mes –
At the beginning of the month

Al final del mes – *At the end of the month*

TEST YOURSELF!

Translate the following sentences:

- 'My birthday is on the 27th of September.'

  _____

- 'El primer día de la primavera es el 19 de marzo.'

  _____

- 'October 12th is a national holiday in Spain.'

  _____

- ¿Cuándo vas a ir a la Sede Central de las Naciones Unidas?'
  ¿El dos de junio?'

  _____

PRACTICE EXAM QUESTION

Planning a party

Read the following Facebook message from a friend and answer the followin
multiple choice questions below by choosing option **A**, **B** or **C**.

¡Hola!

Quería hablar contigo hoy para hablar de los planes para la fiesta de cumpleaños de Mercedes, ¡tenemos que hacerlo bien!

En mi opinión, la fiesta debería ser a principios de septiembre, antes del final de las vacaciones de verano. ¿Qué te parece el primer sábado del mes?

El año pasado, la fiesta de Mercedes fue el veintiuno de septiembre, y todos los invitados estaban de mal humor, porque todos tenían que ir al colegio al día siguiente. Qué desastre, ¿no?

De todos modos, necesitamos contratar a un DJ al final de la próxima semana, ¿cuánto nos vamos a gastar? Tenemos un presupuesto reducido, y necesitamos comprar muchas cosas, comida, decoraciones y todo eso.

También voy a visitar el hermano de Mercedes para pedirle su opinión. ¿Te gustaría venir conmigo el día dieciocho a mediodía? Allí podemos concretar nuestros planes. Tengo sólo un objetivo: ¡pasar una velada inolvidable!

Besos,

Julieta

Question 1

Julieta thinks that Mercedes's party should take place:

   a. At the beginning of September

   b. In the middle of September

   c. At the end of September

Question 2

Why would Julieta prefer this time of year?

   a. It would still be summer weather

   b. She would have returned from her holiday

   c. It would be before the end of the summer holidays

Question 3

Last year, Mercedes's party was held on the…

   a. 19th of September

   b. 20th of September

   c. 21st of September

Question 4

Why were all of the guests in a bad mood?

    a. Because they had been at school that day

    b. Because they had to go to school the next day

    c. There were too many people from school there

Question 5

When does Julieta say the DJ has to be booked by?

    a. By the week before the party

    b. By the end of next week

    c. By the end of next month

Question 6

When does Julieta plan to visit Mercedes' brother?

    a. At noon on the 18th

    b. At noon on the 19th

    c. At 12am on the 18th

(Answers are provided at the end of the book).

SEASONS AND WEATHER

his basic vocabulary will most likely pop up in an exam, and will be vital for
iscussing plans and events in a writing task about holidays.

| La primavera | El verano | El otoño | El invierno |

Qué tiempo hace?

| lueve | ➟ | It's raining |
| ieva | ➟ | It's snowing |

ace calor	➟	It's hot
ace frío	➟	It's cold
ace fresco	➟	It's chilly
ace viento	➟	It's windy
ace buen tiempo	➟	The weather is nice
ace mal tiempo	➟	The weather is bad
ace sol	➟	It's sunny

> **TOP TIP!**
>
> Note that these types of weather are formed using the third-person form of the verb '*hacer*', which literally means 'to do' or 'to make'.

Hay nubes	➜	*It's cloudy*
Hay truenos	➜	*There's thunder*
Hay relámpagos	➜	*There's lightning*
Hay niebla	➜	*It's foggy*
Hay neblina	➜	*It's misty*
Hay granizo	➜	*It's hailing*

> **TOP TIP!**
>
> Note that these types of weather are formed using '*hay*', which literally means 'there is' or 'there are'.

WEATHER WARNINGS!

Una tormenta	Un huracán	Un tsunami	Una inundación	Un rayo
A storm	*A hurricane*	*A tsunami*	*A flood*	*A lightning bolt*

MY LIFE

Now that the more basic stuff is out of the way, we are now going to mov
on to slightly harder Spanish words and phrases, and get started with th
module content itself!

Refer to this chapter as a reminder of how to correctly present yourself (usefu
for the speaking exam), describe your relationships with your family, expres
your hopes for the future, and go into detail about your daily routine, includin
discussing the theme of 'healthy living' more generally.

These topics are directly mentioned in the syllabus and will definitely crop u
in an exam, so revise them thoroughly!

DESCRIBING YOURSELF

Learning how to introduce yourself has probably been a staple of you
Spanish study from Year 7, but of course, at GCSE level, you will need t
develop a stronger vocabulary and learn more advanced expressions i
order to impress examiners.

Let's start with the basics, though:

Soy/Me llamo ➜	*I am/my name is…*
Tengo…años ➜	*I am…years old*
(Yo) soy estudiante ➜	*I am a student*
(Yo) vivo en… ➜	*I live in…*
Estoy interesado/a en ➜	*I am interested in…*
Me gusta vestir/llevar… ➜	*I like to wear…*

SAMPLE SPEAKING EXAM RESPONSE

¡Preséntate!

SPANISH

Me presento. Me llamo Felipe y tengo dieciséis años. Mi cumpleaños es en el verano, el veinte de agosto. Soy estudiante del Colegio Safa San José en Getafe, en el sur de Madrid. Vivo con mi familia en una casa adosada cerca del colegio. Soy deportista, juego en un club de fútbol que se reúne dos veces por semana para entrenar y competir. También **estoy interesado** en la actuación, y me gusta participar en las producciones teatrales de mi colegio.

En cuanto a mi personalidad, **me considero una persona atenta y amable**. Además, mi familia dice que soy extrovertido porque me encanta salir con mis amigos. **Sin embargo**, ¡mi novia Marisol opina que soy demasiado hablador! Aun así, soy bastante trabajador y me tomo en serio mis estudios. Aunque eso sí, se puede decir que paso demasiado tiempo en el gimnasio – durante las vacaciones escolares y el fin de semana, ¡**estoy allí** todo el tiempo!

Note the variety of verb tenses and grammatical structures, relevant vocabulary, and ways of expressing your opinions. Of course, showing you can use a variety of constructions and elements of grammar will maximise your marks!

estoy interesado – **Past participle**

Me considero – **Opinions**

atenta y amable – **Relevant vocabulary/Adjectives**

Sin embargo – **Adverb**

estoy allí – **Present Simple**

TRANSLATION:

Introduce yourself!

<u>ENGLISH</u>

Let me introduce myself. My name is Felipe and I am 16 years old. My birthday is in summer, on the 20th of August. I am a student at the Safa San José School in Getafe, in South Madrid. I live with my family in a semi-detached house close to the school. I am sporty – I play in a football team that meets twice a week to train and compete. I am also interested in acting, and I like taking part in drama productions at school.

In terms of personality, I consider myself as a kind and thoughtful person. Furthermore, my family says that I am extroverted, because I love going out with my friends. However, my girlfriend Marisol thinks that I am too talkative! Even so, I am fairly hardworking, and take my studies seriously. Although, you could say that I spend too much time in the gym – during the school holidays and at weekends, I'm there all the time!

FAMILY AND RELATIONSHIPS

Questions surrounding family situations and relationships invariably come up in exams, and vocabulary surrounding this topic is of course helpful for real-word application. See below for key words presented in a family tree.

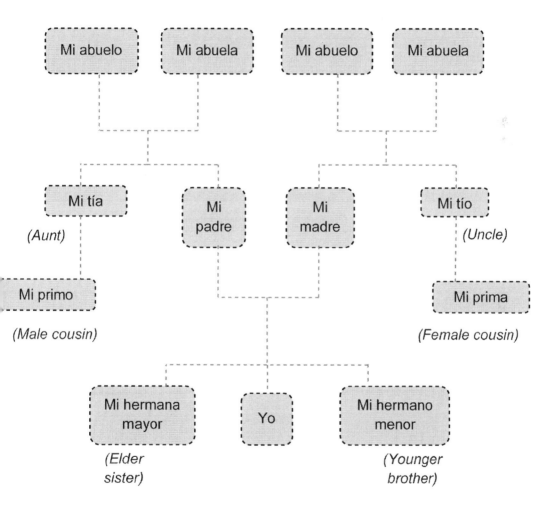

More Vocabulary

El hogar	→	*The household*
Una familia monoparental	→	*Single-parent family*
El hijo	→	*Son*
La hija	→	*Daughter*
Los gemelos/Las gemelas	→	*Twins*
El único hijo/La única hija	→	*Only child*
El hermanastro/La hermanastra	→	*Step-brother/Step-sister*
El padrastro	→	*Step-father*
La madrastra	→	*Step-mother*
El sobrino/La sobrina	→	*Nephew/Niece*

Describing Family Relationships

LO POSITIVO	LO NEGATIVO
Tengo una buena relación con... *I have a good relationship with...*	**Tengo una relación difícil con...** *I have a difficult relationship with...*
Me llevo bien con... *I get on well with...*	**Me llevo mal con...** *I don't get on with...*
Me siento apoyado *I feel supported*	**Me critican demasiado** *They criticise me too much*
Confío en *I trust...*	**Discutimos a menudo** *We often argue*
Atento/Atenta a mis necesidades *Attentive to my needs*	**Una falta de comprensión** *A lack of understanding*
Me cae bien...(una persona) *I like... (a person)*	**Se burla de mí** *He/She mocks me*
Compartimos los mismos intereses *We share the same interests*	**Un choque de personalidades** *A personality clash*
Nos divertimos juntos *We have fun together*	**Comportamiento molesto** *Irritating behaviour*

PRACTICE EXAM QUESTION

My family life

Read the conversation between these students who are discussing the home lives. Answer the questions below **in English**.

Dorotea: Ya no soporto más vivir en mi casa. Soy hija única y no me gusta serlo porque mis padres son sobreprotectores conmigo. Peleamos mucho porque yo no tengo ninguna independencia y ellos son demasiado estrictos. Por ejemplo, la semana pasada no me permitieron ir a una fiesta con mis amigos ¡porque había chicos invitados! Tanta falta de comprensión. Si pudiera mudarme, ¡lo haría!

Leonardo: En general, estoy contento en casa. Vivo con mi padre, mi hermano gemelo, y mi hermana mayor. Me llevo bien con todo el mundo, y todos me han apoyado siempre en todos los aspectos de mi vida – mi padre es gracioso y es mi modelo. Mis hermanos y yo también tenemos muchos intereses en común. ¿Mi única queja? ¡No soy siempre el centro de atención!

Mauricio: Soy el mayor de los cuatro chicos de mi familia – tengo dieciséis años y mi hermano menor tiene ocho años. He tenido que hacerme cargo de muchas de las responsabilidades domésticas para ayudar a mi madre soltera. Por ejemplo, cocino las comidas y hago las compras. Jamás cuestiono la situación porque mi madre necesita ayuda, es así de simple. Además, nos llevamos mal con nuestro padre.

Ivana: Para mí, la vida familiar tiene sus altibajos. Vivo con mi madre, mi padrastro y su hijo (mi hermanastro) que es un chico callado. Nuestra nueva familia fue creada después de la separación de mis padres, y al principio estaba muy triste. No me llevaba bien con mi padrastro, porque lo consideraba como un intruso. Pero, desde entonces, me he dado cuenta de que no ha hecho nada malo.

Question 1

What two reasons does Dorotea give for the frequent arguments with her parents?

Question 2

How many members of his family is Leonardo on good terms with?

Question 3

How many older brothers does Mauricio have?

Question 4

How did Ivana feel about her newly formed family situation at first?

Question 5

Why wasn't Dorotea allowed to go to the party?

Question 6

Leonardo describes his father as being his role model, and shares man[y] interests with his siblings, but what complaint does he give?

Question 7

Why doesn't Mauricio ever question his responsibilities?

Question 8

How did Ivana initially perceive her stepfather?

(Answers are provided at the end of the book).

Relationships and hopes for the future

You may think that talking about relationships is an odd choice of topic for a GCSE syllabus, but as you probably know, discussing hopes and plans for the future is a common subject to come up in an oral exam situation.

Mi novio/novia ideal…
My ideal boyfriend/girlfriend…

me haría feliz
would make me happy

me daría apoyo/me apoyaría
would give me support

sería fiel
would be loyal

tendría su propia independencia
would have their own independence

debería tener un buen sentido del humor
should have a good sense of humour

sería romántico/romántica
would be romantic

Para mí, una mala pareja
For me, a bad partner…

me pondría nervioso/nerviosa
would make me anxious

sería demasiado egoísta
would be too selfish

pasaría demasiado tiempo en las redes sociales
would spend too much time on social media

sería perezoso/perezosa
would be lazy

tendría actitudes inmaduras
would be immature

no me haría sentir especial
wouldn't make me feel special

Romantic plans for the future:

- **Quiero casarme** – *I intend to marry*

- **No deseo establecerme** – *I have no desire to settle down*

- **Espero enamorarme** – *I hope to fall in love*

- **Me gustaría formar una familia en el futuro** – *I would like to start family in the future*

- **No lo he pensado todavía; en este momento mi prioridad es logra mi admisión en la universidad** – *I have not thought about it yet; at th moment my priority is getting into university*

Key phrases

Quedarse soltero/soltera – *Staying single*

La boda – *Wedding*

El matrimonio civil – *Civil marriage*

El matrimonio entre personas del mismo sexo –*Same-sex marriage*

La unión civil – *Civil partnership*

La vida en común – *Living together*

El compromiso – *Engagement*

Sentirse atraído/atraída
To feel attracted

Enamorarse
To fall in love

El flechazo
Love at first sight

Coquetear
To flirt

El cariño
Affection

DAILY ROUTINE

Another regular speaking exam scenario is a conversation about daily routine. A common way this could manifest itself is in the form of the prompt: 'Describe a normal day'.

See below for a sample response and its translation, but without the verbs conjugated! In the Spanish version, fill in the correct forms of the verbs given in the paragraphs below. Note that many of them are reflexive!

1. despertarse	**2.** levantarse	**3.** quedarse
4. ducharse	**5.** cepillarse	**6.** vestirse
7. tomar	**8.** salir	**9.** llegar
10. volver	**11.** relajarse	**12.** ayudar
13. arreglar	**14.** hacer	**15.** preparar
16. acostarse	**17.** conectarme	**18.** dormirse

¡Hola! Voy a describirte en qué consiste un día normal para mí. En primer lugar, cada día _____ a las siete de la mañana, pero no _____ hasta las siete y media – me gusta _____ en la cama un rato. Después, _____. Si se me hace tarde, _____ los dientes al mismo tiempo. Después, _____ _____ el desayuno – normalmente como unas tostadas y bebo café. Ahora, ya estoy listo para _____ de casa.

La mayoría de las veces, _____ temprano al colegio para no llegar tarde cuando pasan lista. Me gusta ser puntual porque mi profesora parece no tener ¡ningún sentido del humor con los tardones!

Así que, al final de una larga jornada escolar, _____ a casa a las cuatro de la tarde para disfrutar de algo de tiempo libre. Normalmente, en cuanto llego a casa lo primero que hago es encender la televisión y _____ un rato. Mis

programas de televisión favoritos son las comedias, podría verlas durant
horas. Sin embargo, no puedo hacer el vago tanto; también debo _____
con las tareas domésticas.

Primero, tengo que _____ el salón si está desordenado, y sacar a pasea
al perro. Después, me siento para _____ los deberes – ¡mis profesores m
mandan un montón de tareas! Y por último, debo _____ la cena para I
familia, aunque esto es algo que me encanta hacer.

Por fin, _____ a las diez de la noche. Pero, _____ por internet en I
cama cada noche – ¡me gusta pasar alrededor de una hora en Twitter
YouTube antes de _____!

(Answers are provided at the end of the book).

TRANSLATION

Hello! I am going to describe what a normal day is for me. Firstly, I wake u
at 7 o'clock every day, although I do not get up until half past seven becaus
I like to stay in bed for a while. Then I take a shower – if I am late, I brush m
teeth at the same time! Afterwards, I get dressed and then, I have breakfast
usually I eat some toast and drink coffee. Now, I am ready to leave the house

Most of the time, I arrive at school slightly early to avoid being late fo
registration. I like to be on time because my teacher does not have a goo
sense of humour when it comes to lateness!

So, after a long school day, I return home at about 4pm and enjoy some fre
time. Usually, as soon as I get home, I turn on the TV and relax for a while
My favourite shows to watch are sitcoms – I could spend hours watchin
them. However, I cannot spend the whole evening being lazy; I must also hel
around the house.

First, it's up to me to tidy up the living room if it's messy, and take my do
for a walk. Then, I sit down to do some homework – school gives me loads
And lastly, I must prepare dinner for the family, although this is something
love to do.

Finally, I go to bed at around 10. But, I always browse Internet in bed – I lik
spending around an hour on Twitter and YouTube before falling asleep!

LIVING HEALTHILY

The topic of healthy living is a very important one, as there is a vast array of ways your knowledge could be tested by examiners. Questions about diet, exercise and stress, as well as alcohol and drugs, may well appear in all four of your Spanish exams, so make sure you have an extensive 'Living Healthily' vocabulary at your fingertips!

Let's start with some helpful phrases:

Una dieta sana	A healthy diet
Un régimen equilibrado	A balanced diet
Alimentos sanos	Healthy food
Los alimentos calóricos	High-calorie foods
Dañino para la salud	Bad for your health
Un estilo de vida no saludable	An unhealthy lifestyle
Un peligro para la salud	Health hazard
La vida sedentaria	Sedentary lifestyle
La epidemia de obesidad	The obesity epidemic
La enfermedad cardíaca	Heart disease

Verbos Útiles!

Engordar	→	To put on weight
Quemar grasa	→	To burn fat
Vigilar el peso	→	To watch one's weight
Cuidarse la línea	→	To watch your figure

Perder peso	→	*To lose weight*
Mantenerse en forma	→	*To keep fit*
Llevar una vida sana	→	*To lead a healthy life*
Estar saludable	→	*To be healthy*
Tener sobrepeso	→	*To be overweight*

*¿Cuánto énfasis pones en la salud? Personalmente creo **la vida sana** lo es todo. Siempre **como sano**; no soporto la comida rápida. Me aseguro de que el ejercicio forma parte de **mi rutina diaria**.*

*Jaja, soy todo lo contrario. Trato de **mantener un régimen equilibrado**, pero me gusta disfrutar de **mis comidas favoritas** – la pizza y la masa de galletas. Pero eso sí, tengo que hacer **más ejercicio**.*

PRACTICE EXAM QUESTION

Gorda Bretaña

Read the following article about health trends in the UK. Answer the questions below **in English**.

Según la Organización de las Naciones Unidas para la Alimentación y la Agricultura, el Reino Unido tiene las tasas más altas de obesidad en Europa Occidental. Estadísticas oficiales muestran que un 24,9% de la población británica está considerada 'obesa', y advertían que esa cifra podría aumentar hasta un cincuenta por ciento en 2050.

Sin duda representa un problema grave, pero ¿cuáles son las causas? Podíamos decir que la culpa la tiene nuestro estilo de vida moderno, que depende en gran medida de los coches, internet, y la comida rápida. De hecho, nuestras vidas son cada vez más sedentarias, y los riesgos para la salud cada vez más omnipresentes.

Así que está claro que como nación, necesitamos considerar nuestros hábitos y tratar de convertirnos en una sociedad más activa, más responsable, más sana, y más feliz. No podemos permitirnos el continuar por este camino tan dañino para nuestra salud. Pero ¿cómo podemos lograr esto? Debemos adoptar una doble estrategia. Por un lado, se necesita que el gobierno tome una serie de medidas prácticas, y por otro lado, todos deberíamos tratar de tomar mejores decisiones personales con respecto a nuestra salud.

En primer lugar, el gobierno debería imponer sanciones duras contra los excesos alcohólicos, y subir los impuestos sobre el tabaco. El alcohol y los cigarrillos no sólo contribuyen a aumentar en gran medida la obesidad, sino que también las enfermedades hepáticas y pulmonares cuestan al NHS millones de libras al año. Además, para animar a los jóvenes a hacer más deporte, deberían reducir los precios de los gimnasios y de los clubs de deporte.

Por otra parte, la población también debería ser proactiva al elegir un estilo de vida saludable. Por ejemplo, sería aconsejable incrementar el consumo diario de frutas y verduras, y dormir bien y aprender a gestionar el estrés para ayudar a controlar el aumento de peso.

En resumen, la obesidad es uno de los problemas sanitarios más importantes en el mundo moderno, y para hacerle frente, todos debemos actuar con decisión – en caso contrario, nos veremos abocados a un desastre.

Question 1

What does the Food and Agriculture Organisation of the United Nations sa about the UK? Mention **one** of the points discussed in the text.

Question 2

According to the second paragraph, what **two** aspects of our moder lifestyles are to blame?

Question 3

According to the third paragraph, what can we **not** do?

Question 4

Out of the three mentioned, name **two specific actions** the government should take, according to the fourth paragraph.

Question 5

Apart from eating more fruits and vegetables, what else is said to help slow down weight gain? Write the **two** points mentioned in the fifth paragraph.

Question 6

Summarise the message of the final paragraph.

DRINKING AND DRUG USE

Una bebida alcohólica ➡ Alcoholic drink

Hacer botellón ➡ *(Something of a Spanish cultural tradition, 'el botellón' involves gathering outside to drink with friends)*

Perder las inhibiciones ➡ To lose one's inhibitions

Estar borracho/a ➡ To be drunk

Abuso del alcohol ➡ Alcohol abuse

Una droga **Un narcótico**	*A drug*
Una droga blanda	*A soft drug*
Las drogas duras	*Hard drugs*
Un terreno resbaladizo	*A slippery slope*
Volverse adicto/adicta	*To become addicted*
Engancharse	*To get hooked on*
Un drogadicto **Un toxicómano**	*A drug addict*
Apoyo del gobierno	*Government support*
Un programa de rehabilitación	*Rehabilitation programme*

En mi opinión

Introducing opinions!

En mi opinión, las personas deberían poder decidir si quieren tomar drogas.

En mi opinión/A mi parecer...
In my opinion...

Estoy convencido/a de que...
I am convinced

Estoy convencido de que deberían existir algunas leyes antinarcóticos.

Tengo que confesar que...
I must admit that...

No estoy ni a favor ni en contra de...
I am neither in favor nor against...

Acepto de manera inequívoca que todos los consumidores de drogas son criminales peligrosos.

No estoy de acuerdo con...
I do not agree with...

Refuto el argumento de que/ Rechazo el argumento de que...
I reject the argument that...

Match the above opinions to their English translations by writing 1, 2 o 3 in the corresponding boxes below:

> I accept unequivocally that all drug addicts are dangerous criminals.

> In my opinion, people should be able to decide whether they want to take drugs.

> I'm certain that some anti-drug laws should exist.

LEISURE
AND
NEW MEDIA

The next module topic is 'Leisure and New Media'. In this chapter, we ar
going to look at Spanish terminology used for talking about free time in mor
detail. This chapter will also cover the subject of 'new technology', i.e. th
Internet and smartphones.

As you know, these subjects will potentially appear in all four of you
assessments, so let's get started.

Although we touched upon this topic when looking at daily routine, 'Fre
Time' deserves a section of its own, as examiners love making you talk abou
it in speaking and writing exams. So, having some phrases and vocab in you
back pocket is very advisable.

FREE TIME

Mis aficiones/pasatiempos	My hobbies
Mis gustos musicales	My music tastes
Mi deporte preferido	My favourite sport
Mis programas favoritos	My favourite programmes
Videojuegos	Video games
Reunirse con amigos	To get together with friends
Salir	To go out

Los días de la semana/Entre semana → *On weekdays*

Los fines de semana → *On weekends*

Soy muy activo/a en mi tiempo libre → *I am very active in my free tim*

En cuanto a mí, prefiero relajarme → *As for me, I prefer to relax*

No hay instalaciones → *There is a lack of facilities*

No hay nada que hacer → *There's nothing to do*

No se da prioridad a los jóvenes → *Young people are not prioritised*

PRACTICE EXAM QUESTION

My hobbies

Read the conversation between these British students who are discussing what they like to do in their free time. Answer the questions below by circling either **TRUE**, **FALSE** or **NOT MENTIONED**.

Archie: Mi tiempo libre siempre ha estado ocupado por el deporte y la música. Soy miembro de un equipo de baloncesto, y competimos a nivel nacional. Así que dedico muchas horas de la semana a entrenar, y también me paso casi todo el fin de semana entrenando. Aparte del baloncesto, la música también es muy importante para mí. Gracias a ella, puedo desconectarme del mundo y relajarme.

Thomas: Paso al menos dos horas al día en el skatepark de mi ciudad. A mí nunca me gustó el fútbol – el skate es mi pasión. Pero antes de que construyeran el skatepark el año pasado, mis compañeros y yo no teníamos ningún sitio donde hacer lo que nos gusta – teníamos que patinar en la calle. No hace falta decir que la gente del barrio estaba muy enfadada con nosotros. Pero ahora todo va bien.

Sophie: Estoy muy interesada en los videojuegos, y dedico una gran parte de mi tiempo libre a jugar con mi consola. ¿Mi género favorito? Son los juegos de tiro o los puzzles, pero me gusta probarlo todo. Con mi PlayStation me conecto a internet para encontrarme con mis amigos. Podemos charlar y jugar juntos, ¡es genial!

Max: En cuanto a mí, soy un lector asiduo. Fuera del colegio, devoro un libro por semana – normalmente, elijo una novela americana o algo de Federico García Lorca. Por otro lado, nunca veo la televisión; lo considero una pérdida de tiempo. Pero me encanta visitar museos y paso cada fin de semana en una galería de arte. Empaparme de cultura de calidad es mi vida.

Question 1

Archie uses basketball to switch off and relax.

TRUE	FALSE	NOT MENTIONED

Question 2

Skating is Tom's passion.

TRUE	FALSE	NOT MENTIONED

Question 3

Sophie hates gaming on her PC.

TRUE	FALSE	NOT MENTIONED

Question 4

Max likes watching television.

TRUE	FALSE	NOT MENTIONED

Question 5

On weekdays, Archie spends many hours training.

TRUE	FALSE	NOT MENTIONED

Question 6

Tom started skating when the skatepark was built in his town.

TRUE	FALSE	NOT MENTIONED

Question 7

Videogames play a role in Sophie's social life.

TRUE	FALSE	NOT MENTIONED

Question 8

Max loves immersing himself in high culture.

TRUE	FALSE	NOT MENTIONED

(Answers are provided at the back of the book).

FASHION

This may seem like a niche topic, but it is a useful gateway into subjects suc as youth culture and self-expression. Relevantly and accurately discussin wider concepts like this in writing and speaking exams is guaranteed to boos your marks, as you may not have been specifically prompted to do so.

Showing examiners that you can take the initiative in this way is a great wa to impress them, as long as doing so makes sense for the question!

Basic Vocab

La ropa – *Clothes*	**Pantalones vaqueros/Jeans** – *Jeans*
Una camisa – *A shirt*	**Una falda** – *A skirt*
Una camiseta – *A t-shirt*	**Los zapatos** – *Shoes*

El corte de pelo/El peinado	*Hairstyle*
El maquillaje	*Makeup*
Un vestido	*A dress*
Un traje	*A suit*
El tatuaje	*Tattoo*
El piercing	*Piercing*

Going Further

seguir la moda	➝	*To follow fashion*
la ropa de marca	➝	*Designer clothes*
las marcas más demandadas	➝	*The most popular brands*
estar muy de moda	➝	*To be fashionable/in fashion*
las últimas tendencias	➝	*The newest trends*

la autoexpresión – *Self-expression*

Un aspecto importante de la identidad de los jóvenes – *An important part of youth identity*

la cultura juvenil – *Youth culture*

Me gusta distinguirme de los demás/Me gusta diferenciarme de los demás – *I like to distinguish myself from others*

SAMPLE SPEAKING EXAM RESPONSE

¿Cómo gastas el dinero?

Me llamo Julio, y **voy a decirte** como gasto mi dinero. Mis padres me dan diez euros cada semana, a cambio de hacer algunas tareas domésticas.

Para mí es un gran placer salir a comprar ropa. Tengo pasión por la moda, y utilizo una gran parte de mi dinero para añadir cosas nuevas a mi colección de zapatillas, joyería y camisas. Es importante para mí estar al día de las **últimas tendencias**.

Aunque es verdad que prefiero productos de marca, **estoy en contra de aquellos que piensan que es superficial**. En mi vida, la moda representa una forma importante de expresión, **sin la cual** yo perdería mi identidad.

Note the variety of verb tenses and grammatical structures, relevant vocabulary, and expressions used to give your opinion! Of course, showing you can use a variety of constructions and elements of grammar will maximise your marks!

voy a decirte – immediate future tense

últimas tendencias – relevant vocab

estoy en contra – personal opinions

sin la cual – relative pronoun

Translation:

How do you spend money?

My name is Julio, and I am going to tell you how I spend my money. My parents give me ten euros every week, in exchange for doing some household chores.

So, going shopping for clothes is a great pleasure for me. Fashion is my passion, and I use a large part of my money to add new things to my collection of trainers, jewellery and shirts. It's important to me to keep up to date with the newest trends.

While it's true that I prefer branded clothes, I am against the view that this equates to superficiality. In my life, fashion represents an important way of expression, without which I would lose my identity.

Here there is some space for you to answer the question: "¿Qué importancia tiene la moda en tu vida?" in the context of a speaking exam response.

DIRECTIONS, TRAVEL AND HOLIDAYS

Being able to speak about forms of transport and tourism is very useful at any level, and some knowledge of vocabulary about these subjects is almost guaranteed to be tested in at least one of your exams.

Of course, confidence in this regard will also be indispensable when you find yourself in a Spanish-speaking country, as you will be better prepared for getting yourself around!

Basic Directions

There are a few common ways of asking directions in Spanish, which thankfully are all fairly simple!

- **Perdón, ¿dónde está el ayuntamiento, por favor? –**

Excuse me, where is the town hall, please?

- **¿Cómo puedo llegar a la estación de tren? –**

How do I get to the train station?

- **¿Por dónde se va al estadio? –**

How do you get to the stadium?

Basic responses to these types of questions could include:

'Desde aquí...' – 'From here...'

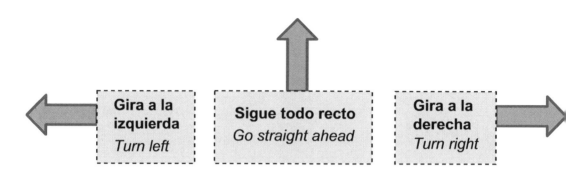

| Gira a la izquierda
Turn left | **Sigue todo recto**
Go straight ahead | Gira a la derecha
Turn right |

¡Cuidado! Another way of saying '**go straight ahead**' is '***sigue todo derecho***' which, as you can see, uses the word for 'right' in it. So, be careful you are not hearing 'go right' when what you're being told is 'go straight on'!

More instructions to do with following directions:

Al final de la calle → *At the end of the street*

A la vuelta de la esquina → *Around the corner*

Al lado de... → *Next to...*

Ve/Coge/Cruza → *Go/Take/Cross [informal 'tú' version]*

Está lejos → *It's far away*

Está cerca → *It's close by*

Getting Around Locally

A pie → *On foot*

En bicicleta → *By bike*

En autobús → *By bus*

En tren → *By train*

En coche → *By car*

En taxi → *By taxi*

En metro	→	*By metro/underground*
En tranvía	→	*By tram*

Medios de transporte	→	*Transport networks*
Seguro/Fiable	→	*Reliable*
Insuficiente	→	*Insufficient*

Travelling Abroad

Un viaje	*A trip/journey*
Una estancia	*A stay*
El transporte aéreo de bajo coste	*Budget air travel/Low cost travel*
El aeropuerto	*The airport*
A tiempo/En hora/Puntual	*On time*
Retrasado/a	*Delayed*
Cancelado/a	*Cancelled*
La aduana/El control de pasaportes	*Customs/Passport Control*
Puerta (de embarque)	*Gate*

Holidays

Reservar un hotel	→	*To book a hotel*
Un veraneante/Un turista	→	*A holidaymaker*
Una habitación de hotel	→	*A hotel room*

Un paquete de vacaciones → *A holiday package*

Un complejo vacacional → *A holiday resort*

Una estación de esquí → *A ski resort*

Una escapada → *A getaway*

Vacaciones en plena naturaleza → *Holidays in the heart of nature*

Turismo activo → *Activity holidays*

Una escapada urbana → *A city break*

Un crucero → *A cruise*

¡Países Hispanohablantes!

Argentina	Honduras
Bolivia	México
Chile	Nicaragua
Colombia	Panamá
Costa Rica	Paraguay
Cuba	Perú
Ecuador	Puerto Rico
El Salvador	República Dominicana
España	Uruguay
Guatemala	Venezuela
Guinea Ecuatorial	

Razones para viajar

Relajarse	➡	*To relax*
Descubrir	➡	*To discover*
Hacer turismo	➡	*To go sightseeing*
Divertirse	➡	*To have fun*
Lograr una experiencia auténtica	➡	*To have an authentic experience*
Vivir como un local	➡	*To live like a local*

*Lo que **me motiva** a viajar es **experimentar la cultura local**, y conocer vidas diferentes a la mía. Lo que realmente merece la pena en la vida es **viajar por el mundo**.*

*Por mi parte, suelo **irme de vacaciones** para **desconectar del estrés diario**. Si me lleva a un lugar cálido con piscina, **me haría feliz**.*

*Personalmente, me gusta **ir al extranjero para estar activa**. Me encanta la escalada en roca, hacer rappel y el ciclismo de montaña, cosas para las que **no tengo mucho tiempo***

PRACTICE EXAM QUESTION

The Evolution of Tourism

Read the following article about emerging trends in the travel industry and answer the questions below, **in English**.

Nuevos estudios realizados por sitios web de viajes indican que durante el año pasado, las escapadas urbanas fueron por primera vez tan populares como las vacaciones en la playa. La popularidad de esto tipo de turismo ha aumentado dramáticamente entre los británicos a lo largo de los últimos años, con más estancias cortas reservadas cada primavera, verano y otoño.

Esta nueva tendencia puede ser explicada teniendo en cuenta numerosos factores. Primeramente, el pueblo británico se ha vuelto más aventurero a la hora de elegir sus destinos turísticos, abandonando sus 'segundas residencias' en España para descubrir nuevos países.

Además, la industria de las aerolíneas de bajo coste ha experimentado un crecimiento espectacular, y hoy en día es posible viajar a una amplia gama de destinos sin pagar una fortuna. Así que, los turistas han empezado a aprovechar esta oportunidad con gran alegría. Por ejemplo, actualmente la tendencia es subirse a un avión en una ciudad europea, hacer un tour por el continente, y volver a casa vía un aeropuerto diferente.

Por último, los jóvenes han tenido una influencia notable en la situación. La revolución de la cultura del smartphone ha dado lugar al turista superinformado – alguien que tiene toda la información al alcance de la mano – literalmente. Esto ha generado un aumento del turismo hacia lugares considerados como destinos 'no tradicionales', tales como Cracovia, Polonia y Tallin, Estonia.

Question 1

What does the first paragraph indicate about the popularity of city breaks compared to beach holidays these days?

Question 2

How have British tourists' behaviour changed according to paragraph 2?

Question 3

According to paragraph 3, how has the air travel industry changed?

Question 4

According to paragraph 4, what has given rise to the hyper-informed tourist?

Question 5

Look back to the first paragraph. How has the increase in popularity of city breaks manifested itself?

Question 6

Considering the article as a whole, what are the **three** specific reasons for the increase in popularity of city breaks?

(Answers are provided at the back of the book).

TV AND CINEMA

Although we have already covered 'free time', the topic of TV and cinema could be the specific focus of your writing or speaking exam.

Also, specific vocabulary on this subject will most likely be required to successfully navigate the listening and reading exams.

Las noticias	*The news*
El pronóstico del tiempo	*The weather forecast*
Una telenovela	*A soap*
Un programa de juegos	*A game show*
Una comedia/sitcom	*A sitcom*
Los dibujos animados	*Cartoons*
El mando (a distancia) **El control remoto**	*The remote control*
Delante de la pantalla	*In front of the screen*
Darse un atracón de Netflix	*To go on a Netflix binge*

Advertising

La publicidad   ➡   *Advertising/Publicity*

Un anuncio   ➡   *An advert/advertisement/ad*

Los anuncios de televisión me enojan	TV adverts annoy me
Están por todas partes	They are everywhere
Estamos siendo bombardeados	We are bombarded
Los anunciantes son a menudo sexistas	Advertisers are often sexist
¿Un mal necesario?	A necessary evil?

¡Un debate!

A mi juicio, el gobierno debe limitar el volumen de publicidad al que estamos expuestos.

En cuanto a mí, yo no lo veo como un problema; los anuncios me proporcionan información útil sobre buenos productos.

No, es una forma de controlar inaceptable – que llevan a cabo las grandes empresas ¡que sólo desean tener mayores beneficios!

¡Nadie te está obligando a gastar tu dinero! Cada uno debe ser capaz de controlarse a sí mismo.

El Cine

Una película...

...de acción	→	An action film
...de aventuras	→	An adventure film
...de terror	→	A horror film
...de ciencia ficción	→	A science fiction film
...de dibujos animados	→	An animation film
...de amor	→	A romantic film
...en habla hispana	→	A film in Spanish
...de Hollywood	→	A Hollywood film
...del Reino Unido	→	A British film

Una comedia – A comedy

Un musical – A musical

Un documental – A documentary

Un drama – A drama

Un thriller – A thriller

Handy Vocab!

Estreno en salas – Theatrical release
Cinéfilo/a – A film buff
Una estrella de cine – A film star
Efectos especiales – Special effects
El/La cineasta – Filmmaker

¡Me considero un gran cinéfilo! Me encanta ir al cine para ver todas las películas taquilleras del momento.

Para mí, ir al cine no está tan mal. Iría con mis amigos si lo sugieren; puedo disfrutar de las películas normales y

Yo odio el cine. Es sofocante, y no puedo llevar mi propia comida. No tengo ninguna razón para ir.

THE INTERNET AND SOCIAL MEDIA

'The Internet' is a topic that is going to appear in language exams in greater depth and with greater frequency as years go by. Of course, more and more Internet vocabulary is coming into practice every day from many languages, much of which causes debate in Spain over how to best translate it.

At GCSE level, exam questions about Internet habits and social media have become almost guaranteed, so make sure you know lots of specialised vocabulary, which you will find below!

Un internauta	An Internet user
Un ordenador	A desktop computer
Un ordenador portátil	A laptop
El teclado	Keyboard
El ratón	Mouse
Una conexión WiFi	A WiFi connection
Un sitio web Una página web	A website A webpage
Un motor de búsqueda	A search engine
Un navegador Un explorador	A browser
(Una dirección de) correo electrónico	An email address

Hacer clic	→	To click
Pulsar una tecla	→	To press a key
Copiar y pegar	→	Copy and paste
Un enlace	→	A link
La clave de acceso/ La contraseña	→	Password

Smartphones

Un smartphone	A smartphone
Una tableta	A tablet
Datos móviles	Mobile data
Navegación a través del móvil	Mobile browsing
Una app	An app
Un cargador de móvil	Phone charger
La duración de la batería	Battery life

Descargar música   ➝   Downloading music

Una descarga   ➝   A download

El streaming/La transmisión   ➝   Streaming

Cargar/Subir un vídeo a YouTube   ➝   Uploading a video to YouTube

Social Media

Las redes sociales	Social media
Una solicitud de amistad	A friend request
Cronología	Timeline
Foto de perfil	Profile picture
Un tweet	A tweet
Una historia Snapchat	A Snapchat story
Un chat grupal/de grupo	A group chat
Un grupo de WhatsApp	A WhatsApp group
Un me gusta/like en Instagram	An Instagram like
Una llamada de Skype	A Skype call

¡Verbos Útiles!

Publicar en Facebook	→	*To post on Facebook*
Tuitear	→	*To tweet*
Reenviar/Retuitear/Retweet	→	*To retweet*
Enviar un mensaje directo	→	*To send a direct message*

Below are some opinions about the benefits and risks of social media and smartphones.

Match the opinions in Spanish to their correct translations by drawing lines, and learn the useful phrases and vocab! The first matches have been made to serve as examples.

Los beneficios

Plataformas como Facebook pueden sensibilizar al público sobre temas importantes.

You can instantly connect with friends to plan an event.

Tener un perfil de internet enseña a los jóvenes a desarrollar sus identidades, y a encontrar una voz propia y personal.

It's easy to share your life's best moments with your friends.

Se puede conectar instantáneamente con amigos para planear un evento.

Platforms like Facebook can raise public awareness about important subjects.

Es fácil compartir los mejores momentos de tu vida con tus amigos.

Social networks are great for keeping in touch with loved ones.

Las redes sociales son perfectas para mantenerse en contacto con los seres queridos.

Having an Internet profile teaches young people to develop their identities and find a distinct voice of their own.

Los riesgos

La creencia de que una obsesión por los smartphones puede generar problemas de salud mental ya es comúnmente aceptada.

It is possible to become addicted to social media, and you can risk losing your connection to the real world.

La exposición a las pantallas brillantes perturba el sueño.

Sharing personal details online could lead to fraud or theft.

Es posible hacerse adicto a las redes sociales, y hay riesgo de perder la conexión con el mundo real.

The belief that an obsession with smartphones can lead to mental health problems is now widely accepted.

Compartir información personal en línea podría dar lugar a fraude o robo.

Irresponsible use of social media could cost you a job in the future.

El uso irresponsable de una red social puede costarte un empleo en el futuro.

Exposure to bright screens disturbs sleep.

(Answers are provided at the back of the book).

SAMPLE WRITING EXAM RESPONSE

Module: Technology

Task: In order to better understand her young constituents and their online lives, a member of your local council has asked you to write to her about young people and the Internet.

She would like you to give opinions on the use of social media in today's society, as well as discuss your own online presence and Internet habits.

Include details of the following:

1. How often you use various social media platforms;
2. Your opinions on the benefits of social media;
3. Your opinions on the 'dark side' of social media: oversharing, bullying, etc.

Estimada Concejala,

Voy a describir mis impresiones sobre el uso de internet por parte de los jóvenes, y discutir sus hábitos en las redes sociales.

En primer lugar, es innegable que hoy en día las vidas sociales de los jóvenes están fuertemente vinculadas a plataformas como Facebook y Twitter. Miles de nuevos usuarios se inscriben en todo tipo de redes cada semana, y apps como Instagram y Snapchat se descargan millones de veces cada día. Internet se ha convertido en el método de comunicación más común entre los jóvenes, y representa una herramienta importante de expresión personal.

Personalmente, me paso varias horas al día navegando por mis páginas de Facebook y Twitter. Me encanta charlar con mis amigos y buscar memes de Internet porque me hacen reír. Además, estoy constantemente conectado a servicios de mensajes como WhatsApp, así que recibo muchas alertas y notificaciones a lo largo del día. Hasta hace muy poco, esto me distraía mucho y yo no era productivo en mi trabajo. Sin embargo, ahora ya he aprendido que a la hora de trabajar, ¡el teléfono debería estar apagado!

Sí, sería justo decir que soy adicta a mi smartphone, y mi experiencia me dice que internet tiene una gran fuerza adictiva sobre la mayoría de los adolescentes. Pero no pienso que este hecho sea necesariamente malo, porque el avance de internet y la poderosa influencia que la nueva tecnología tiene en nuestras vidas sólo pueden beneficiarnos a todos. En concreto, estoy seguro de que la innovación técnica dentro del área de la medicina nunca dejará de sorprendernos.

Tampoco podemos olvidar que las redes sociales aportan claras ventajas que ayudan a los jóvenes en la vida cotidiana. Por ejemplo, la comunicación digital es indispensable en el desarrollo de las relaciones y las amistades. Sin duda, sería muy difícil para un alumno de una escuela secundaria el integrarse en un círculo de amigos sin tener una presencia en línea. Una vez más, no creo que esto revele la superficialidad de la generación moderna; ¡no es culpa suya haber nacido en la era de internet!

A pesar de todo esto, soy consciente de que una conexión constante tiene ciertas desventajas; obviamente, hay un lado oscuro de las redes sociales. Primero, se puede decir que una minoría de jóvenes no las utiliza con suficiente responsabilidad. Es importante tener cuidado acerca de con quién se habla en línea, y saber que el compartir datos personales con extraños podría ponerte en peligro. Igualmente, un desafío importante de nuestro tiempo es ganar la lucha contra el ciberacoso, que tiene capacidad para destruir vidas.

Para concluir, estoy convencido de que los aspectos positivos de Internet tienen más importancia que los elementos negativos. Creo que con educación adecuada sobre seguridad en línea, deberíamos confiar en que los jóvenes actuarán de forma responsable, y darlos la libertad de expresarse, navegar, y hablar como quieren pese a los peligros potenciales.

Le saluda atentamente,

Esteban R.

Note the variety of verb tenses and grammatical structures, relevant vocabulary, and expressing opinions.

es innegable que – Introducing ideas

se ha convertido – Range of tenses

el método más común – Superlatives

esto – Range of pronouns

Sin embargo – Range of adverbs

ya – Range of adverbs

estoy seguro de que – Introducing opinions

dejará – Range of tenses

no creo que...revele – Subjunctive

A pesar de – Range of prepositions

Translation:

Dear Councilmember,

I am going to give you my impressions about how young people use the Internet, and discuss their habits on social media.

Firstly, it is undeniable that today, young people's social lives are strongly linked to online platforms such as Facebook and Twitter. Thousands of new users sign up to all types of these networks every week and apps like Instagram and Snapchat are downloaded millions of times per day. The Internet has become the most common method of communication amongst young people, and it represents an important tool of self-expression.

Personally, I spend several hours a day browsing my Facebook and Twitter pages. I love talking with my friends and searching for Internet memes, because they make me laugh. As well as this, I am constantly connected to messaging services like WhatsApp, so I receive many alerts and notifications throughout the day. Until recently, this often distracted me, and I wasn't working productively. However, I have since learned that when it's time to work, my phone should be switched off!

Yes, I must admit that I am addicted to my smartphone, and my experience tells me that the Internet has an addictive force on most adolescents. However, I do not think that this fact is necessarily a bad one, as the development of the Internet and the powerful influence of new technology in our lives can only benefit us all. More specifically, I am certain that technical innovation in areas such as medicine will continue to amaze us forever.

Also, we cannot forget that social media has clear advantages, or that it helps young people in daily life. For example, digital communication is indispensable in the development of relationships and friendships. Without a doubt, it would be very difficult for a secondary school student to integrate into a circle of friends without any form of online presence. Again, I don't think that this shows the modern generation to be superficial; it is not their fault that they live in the Internet age!

In spite of this, I am aware that being constantly connected is not without its disadvantages; obviously there is a dark side to social media. Firstly, it is possible to say that a minority of young people do not use them with enough responsibility. It's essential to be careful about who you are talking to online, and know that sharing personal details with strangers could put you in danger. Equally, an important challenge of today is winning the fight against online harassment/cyberbullying, which has the potential to destroy lives.

But, in conclusion, I am convinced that the positive elements of the Internet outweigh the negatives. I believe that with proper education about online safety, we should trust that young people will act responsibly, and give them the freedom to express themselves, surf, and talk how they want, despite the potential dangers.

Yours sincerely,

Esteban R.

HOME, SCHOOL AND ENVIRONMENT

Similarly to the topic of the Internet, discussing the environment and your local area requires a fair amount of specific vocabulary.

However, this is a very ideal topic for proving that you can express ideas and opinions in Spanish, so knowing a variety of phrases to do with introducing and justifying opinions will be invaluable in writing and speaking exams.

YOUR LOCAL AREA

northeast	northwest	southeast	southwest
noreste/nordeste	**noroeste**	**sureste/sudeste**	**suroeste/sudoeste**

Una ciudad	A city
Un pueblo	A small town
Una aldea	A village
Un barrio residencial	A suburb
Un vecindario/Un barrio	A neighbourhood
Una urbanización	A housing complex, A residential area
Una zona rural	A rural area
En el campo	In the countryside
En una granja	On a farm

Puntos de referencia *(Landmarks)*

Una estatua	$\longrightarrow$	*A statue*
Un monumento	$\longrightarrow$	*A monument*
La catedral	$\longrightarrow$	*The cathedral*
Un rascacielos	$\longrightarrow$	*A skyscraper*
Ruinas históricas	$\longrightarrow$	*Historic ruins*

Un centro comercial	*A shopping centre*
Grandes almacenes	*Department stores*
Cafés y restaurantes	*Cafés and restaurants*
Museos	*Museums*
Una biblioteca	*A library*
Un cine	*A cinema*
Un polideportivo	*Leisure centre/Sports centre*

Describing Where You Live

Edificios modernos/viejos	$\rightarrow$	*Modern/Old buildings*
Una hermosa ciudad	$\rightarrow$	*A beautiful town*
Una ciudad fea	$\rightarrow$	*An ugly town*
Animado/a, lleno/a de vida	$\rightarrow$	*Lively*
Ruidoso	$\rightarrow$	*Loud*
Tranquilo	$\rightarrow$	*Quiet/Peaceful*
Agradable	$\rightarrow$	*Nice, Friendly*
Impersonal	$\rightarrow$	*Impersonal*

¡Opiniones del área local!

1.

> Personalmente, me agrada vivir en mi **pueblo**. Es una **zona urbana** que te ofrece muchas cosas que hacer, y que tiene un **ambiente animado y lleno de vida**. Y además, hay un parque nacional a menos de veinte kilómetros del centro de la ciudad, al que se puede acceder fácilmente con el coche. **¡Es genial!**

2.

> **Donde yo vivo**, no hay mucho que hacer ni que ver. **No hay** cine, y la selección de tiendas deja mucho que desear. Sin embargo, no todo es malo. **Tengo la suerte de que** muchos de mis amigos viven cerca de mí. Cuando podemos, nos reunimos para divertirnos.

3.

> En mi caso, odio la vida en mi **ciudad**. Mi familia **acaba de mudarse** y todavía no me encuentro a gusto porque no tengo amigos aquí. Además, no me gusta el ambiente del lugar, porque **es ruidoso** y la gente parece fría. **Extraño** el campo y el aire libre.

Match the above opinions about local areas to their correct translations below, by writing 1, 2 or 3 in the corresponding boxes:

> Personally, I like living in my town. It's an urban area that offers many things to do, and it has a vibrant atmosphere. What's more, there's a national park less than twenty kilometres from the town centre, which is easily accessible by car. It's great!

> Me, I hate life in my city. My family has just moved and I am still not comfortable, because I have no friends here. In addition, I do not like the atmosphere of the place, because it is loud and the people seem cold. I miss the countryside and fresh air.

> Where I live, there's not much to do or see. There's no cinema, and the selection of shops leaves much to be desired. Having said that, it's not all bad. I am lucky that many of my friends live close to me. When we can, we get together and have fun.

Problems in Town

El paro **El desempleo**	*Unemployment*
La pobreza	*Poverty*
El problema de los sin techo	*The problem of homelessness*
La falta de trabajo	*A lack of jobs*
La falta de vivienda asequible	*The lack of affordable housing*
Los recortes de financiación	*Funding cuts*
La conducta antisocial	*Antisocial behaviour*
El vandalismo	*Vandalism*
El crimen **El delito**	*Crime*

PRACTICE EXAM QUESTION

Charity

Read the following conversation between these British students who are discussing their attitudes towards poverty and charity. Answer the questions below by circling **TRUE**, **FALSE** or **NOT MENTIONED**.

Jasmine: El paro y la desigualdad social son dos de los problemas más graves de nuestra época. No existen soluciones fáciles, pero todos podemos contribuir a mejorar la sociedad. En primer lugar, tenemos que presionar al gobierno para que destine más fondos a la lucha contra la pobreza. Porque como comunidad, todos debemos contribuir a nivel personal.

Barnaby: A mi juicio, las personas sin hogar sólo se pueden culpar a sí mismos. Nuestro sistema de bienestar es efectivo, y muchos programas han sido puestos en práctica para ayudarlos. Además, pienso que la mendicidad en la calle debería ser ilegal – ¿por qué no tienen empleo? Parece que no quieren trabajar, sino emborracharse y tomar drogas. En mi opinión, necesitan hacer un mayor esfuerzo para superarse.

Yan: Creo que el mero hecho de que exista tanta pobreza es un escándalo nacional. Personalmente no estoy contento con un status quo en el que se da por muertas a millones de personas; sin trabajo, sin comida, sin esperanza. En lo que a mí se refiere, dono dinero a una gran variedad de organizaciones benéficas, pero es responsabilidad del gobierno efectuar un cambio real. Hay que hacer una revisión total del sistema.

Emily: En mi opinión, el público está demasiado inclinado a ignorar la gente pobre. Para la mayoría de la población, los sin techo representan nada más que un inconveniente menor. El asombro ha sido reemplazado por la indiferencia, que ahora es la respuesta normal a este problema. No podemos olvidar que los sin hogar no son estadísticas, sino seres humanos que merecen nuestra ayuda.

Question 1

Jasmine believes that unemployment and social inequality are very importan
issues.

TRUE	FALSE	NOT MENTIONED

Question 2

Barnaby thinks that the welfare system is not up to scratch.

TRUE	FALSE	NOT MENTIONED

Question 3

Yan blames the government for the homelessness and poverty.

TRUE	FALSE	NOT MENTIONED

Question 4

Emily believes people have become desensitised to seeing homeless people
in the street.

TRUE	FALSE	NOT MENTIONED

Question 5

Jasmine thinks that the government should prioritise apprenticeship schemes

TRUE	FALSE	NOT MENTIONED

Question 6

Barnaby thinks that it is possible to be hardworking and homeless.

TRUE	FALSE	NOT MENTIONED

Question 7

Yan wants to see government ministers punished for their inaction.

TRUE	FALSE	NOT MENTIONED

Question 8

Emily believes homelessness is an issue which deserves our attention.

TRUE	FALSE	NOT MENTIONED

(Answers are provided at the back of the book).

THE ENVIRONMENT

The topic of the environment is an absolute favourite of examiners. It is al but guaranteed that you will have to deal with this topic in your listening and reading exams, so make sure you revise the next few pages thoroughly.

Teachers also enjoy setting writing and speaking topics around this subject, so get practising! Let's begin with some vocabulary:

El calentamiento del planeta	*Global warming*
El efecto invernadero	*The greenhouse effect*
El derretimiento de las capas de hielo	*The melting of the ice caps*
La contaminación	*Pollution*
Las fábricas	*Factories*
El consumo excesivo	*Excessive consumption*
Los recursos naturales	*Natural resources*
Malgastar	*To waste*
La basura/Los desechos	*Rubbish/Waste*
La deforestación	*Deforestation*
La extinción de las especies	*The extinction of species*

More key terms:

Gases de escape	→	*Exhaust fumes*
Gases nocivos	→	*Harmful gases*
El tráfico/La circulación	→	*Traffic*
El atasco/El embotellamiento	→	*Traffic jam*
La hora punta	→	*Rush hour*
La lluvia ácida	→	*Acid rain*
El transporte público	→	*Public transport*
Montar en bici(cleta)	→	*Riding a bike*
Las pistas para ciclistas	→	*Cycle lanes*

Una campaña medioambiental	→	*An environmental campaign*
La conservación natural	→	*Nature conservation*
Preservar	→	*To preserve*
Conservar	→	*To keep, to save, to preserve*
Ahorrar	→	*To save*
Reutilizar	→	*To reuse*
Reciclar	→	*To recycle*
Clasificar los residuos	→	*To sort waste*
Una multa	→	*A fine*

¡Un debate!

En lo que a mí respecta, es vergonzoso que el gobierno no haya hecho nada para combatir el calentamiento global. La contaminación está en su nivel más alto, y nadie ha actuado aún. Estoy indignada.

En mi opinión, es muy fácil echar la culpa al gobierno. El medio ambiente es responsabilidad de todos. Los pequeños gestos cotidianos son los que marcan la diferencia.

No estoy de acuerdo. Para la inmensa mayoría, el reciclaje doméstico ha pasado a ser una práctica común, y nada ha cambiado. Los científicos aún señalan un deterioro continuo de la situación.

No entiendo; ¿qué quieres que haga el gobierno? Ha animado a las personas a preocuparse más por el medio ambiente, y ¡se han construido centros de reciclaje por todas partes! Los parlamentarios tienen cosas más importantes en las que centrarse.

Admito que todo esto representa un progreso, pero no se han abordado las causas fundamentales de la contaminación. Es decir, hay que castigar a las empresas cuyas fábricas emitan gases tóxicos, y recompensar a las 'compañías verdes'.

SCHOOL LIFE

When talking about education and work, you must prove you are comfortable giving opinions and discussing ideas in a range of tenses. Talking about future plans is another speaking exam classic, and one that could give you some creative freedom! There are no wrong answers for future plans of course; just make sure your Spanish is spot on.

Los deberes	*Homework*
Las notas	*Grades/Marks*
El horario	*Timetable*
La hora del descanso	*Break*
La hora del almuerzo	*Lunch time*
Un curso obligatorio	*A compulsory course*
Un curso optativo	*An optional course*
Las reglas	*The rules*
Los métodos de enseñanza	*The teaching methods*

¡Me encanta mi vida escolar! He hecho muchos amigos, y el temario me parece interesante. A consecuencia de ello, ¡estoy muy motivado para salir de la cama por la mañana e ir al colegio!

He tenido problemas en la escuela. Las clases son aburridas así que me cuesta concentrarme. No merece la pena esforzarse. Además, no les caigo bien a mis compañeros. Es un fracaso total.

¡Mis asignaturas favoritas!

Lo que me interesa es la biología.

What interests me is Biology.

Estudiar música, eso es lo mío/Lo mío es estudiar música.

Studying music, that's my thing.

A mí me parece que las matemáticas tienen sentido.

Maths makes sense to me.

En inglés, me gusta mucho estudiar a los grandes autores del pasado.

In English, I really like studying the great authors of the past.

Soy bueno en deporte, así que me encantan las clases de educación física.

I'm good at sport, so I love PE lessons.

Las menos favoritas!

No puedo comprender la química.
I cannot understand Chemistry.

No tengo ningún talento artístico.
I have no artistic talent.

La educación religiosa no me interesa en absoluto.
Religious education does not interest me at all.

Me siento obligado/a a aprender las lenguas extranjeras modernas.
I feel obliged to learn Modern Foreign Languages.

Para mí, concentrarme en la informática es una lucha diaria.
For me, concentrating on ICT is a daily battle.

POST-SCHOOL PLANS

Después del colegio/Después de terminar el colegio – *After leaving school*

Quiero... – *I want to...*

Me gustaría lograr buenos resultados en los exámenes – *I would like to get good exam results*

Espero conseguir un buen empleo – *I hope to land a good job*

Pretendo ir a la universidad – *I intend to go to university*

Hacer un curso de aprendizaje/Seguir un curso de formación como aprendiz – *Doing an apprenticeship*

Hacer una carrera – *Doing a degree*

Seguir un programa de formación – *Undertaking a training scheme*

PRACTICE EXAM QUESTION

School life and the future

Read the conversation between these British students who are discussing education and their post-school lives. Answer the questions below **in English**.

Joshua: Mis asignaturas favoritas siempre han sido las ciencias y las matemáticas, y he sacado buenas notas desde la escuela primaria. Actualmente, estoy tratando de solicitar unos cursos con prácticas del sector de la Ingeniería. Después de la secundaria, me veo obteniendo un título de ingeniero de una prestigiosa universidad con miras a conseguir un trabajo en una empresa de alto nivel.

Zara: En el colegio, no me interesaban las materias académicas tradicionales. En su lugar, me centré por completo en la música – me encanta componer y toco varios instrumentos, aunque mi favorito es el saxofón. Por eso, siempre ha sido difícil para mí obtener buenos resultados. ¡Ah! No estoy preocupada, voy a llegar a ser ¡la mejor intérprete de música que el mundo haya visto jamás!

Clive: En cuanto a mí, estoy en el último año de colegio. Diría que soy un estudiante promedio, que puede disfrutar de algunas clases y llevarse bien con los profesores. Sin embargo, no tengo ni idea de qué hacer cuanto a mis planes de carrera. Sinceramente, sólo quiero pensar en mi vida social, no en mi futuro.

Question 1

What does Joshua say about his marks at school?

Question 2

What did Zara choose to prioritise over her studies?

Question 3

What does Clive say about his plans for a future profession?

Question 4

What does Joshua want to do after he gets a degree in Engineering?

Question 5

What is Zara's aspiration?

Question 6

What are Clive's feelings towards thinking about the future?

GRAMMAR

Of course, all the vocab knowledge and insightful opinions in the world mean very little if they cannot be conveyed correctly and with grammatical accuracy. A range of verb tenses and grammatical features have been demonstrated throughout this guide. This section will provide you with easy, quick and simple explanations of the fundamental elements on grammar required for GCSE Spanish.

Nouns

A noun constitutes something that is an **object, a living thing, a person**, as well as something that is a **general concept**.

In Spanish, all nouns have gender – they are either masculine or feminine. Gender determines which of the definite and indefinite articles to use when referring to a certain noun, i.e. when to use *el/la/los/las* for 'the', or *un/una/unos/unas* for 'a'.

Examples:

(Masc.) *El canguro*–	The kangaroo	*Un canguro* – A kangaroo
(Fem.) *La calculadora* –	The calculator	*Una calculadora* – A calculator
(Masc.) *El doctor* –	The doctor	*Un doctor* – A doctor
(Fem.) *La doctora* –	The doctor	*Una doctora* – A doctor
(Masc.) *El sexismo* –	Sexism	

When referring to a masculine noun in the plural, '*el*' becomes '*los*', and when referring to a feminine noun in the plural, '*la*' becomes '*las*'.

Examples:

Los *canguros* → The kangaroos

Las *calculadoras* → The calculators

It may seem that there is no rhyme or reason to assigning genders to nouns in Spanish, but it is possible to become familiar with which types of words are largely masculine, and which are largely feminine. Namely, how a word is spelt can let you know which gender it takes.

Here are the word endings that often betray a noun's gender:

A noun is probably **masculine** if it ends with:		A noun is probably **feminine** if it ends with:	
o	→ *el teléfono*	a	→ *la pregunta*
u	→ *el espíritu*	ción	→ *la situación*
r	→ *el tractor*	sión	→ *la emisión*
n	→ *el régimen*	tad	→ *la libertad*
l	→ *el hotel*	tud	→ *la juventud*
s	→ *el autobús*	dad	→ *la posibilidad*
aje	→ *el lenguaje*	umbre	→ *la incertidumbre*
ma	→ *el problema*		
pa	→ *el mapa*		

Obviously, nouns can be **singular** or **plural**.

Similarly to English, making nouns plural always involves the letter 's'.

If the singular form of the noun **ends with a vowel**, all you need to do to make it plural is **add an 's'**.

For example:

El delito	→	*The crime*
Los delito**s**	→	*The crimes*
Una broma	→	*A joke*
Unas broma**s**	→	*Some jokes*

If the singular form of the noun **ends with a consonant**, you need to add '**es**'.

For example:

Un gol	→	*One goal*
Dos gol**es**	→	*Two goals*
Una actividad	→	*An activity*
Dos actividad**es**	→	*Two activities*

If the singular form of the noun **ends with 'z'**, you need to **remove the 'z' and add 'ces'**.

For example:

Un pez	→	*One fish*
Dos pe**ces**	→	*Two fishes*
Una vez	→	*One time (once)*
Dos ve**ces**	→	*Two times (twice)*

Adjectives

Adjectives are used to describe nouns and pronouns, and in order to be used accurately, they need to agree according to the gender and number of the noun. I.e. the adjective has to match with the noun which it is describing, no matter where in a sentence is placed.

For example:

El muchacho alt**o**   →   The tall guy (masculine singular)

Los muchachos alt**os**   →   The tall guys (masculine plural)

La muchacha alt**a**   →   The tall girl (feminine singular)

Las muchachas alt**as**   →   The tall girls (feminine plural)

Some adjectives change meaning depending on where they are placed in a sentence, i.e. if seen before or after the noun they are describing!

For example:

La gran mujer   →   The great woman

La mujer grande   →   The big woman

Verbs

The present tense

Of course, the present tense is used very commonly to:

- Describe actions occurring at the present time (e.g. The man is running)
- Describe actions that happen regularly (e.g. I practise every week)
- Describe actions that are about to happen in the immediate future (e.g. We're going to leave the house in two hours)

- Describe things that are generally observable (e.g. Squirtle is the bes choice of starter.)

As you know, regular verbs in Spanish are said to belong to three main group: that follow set patterns of conjugation. It is possible to work out which group a verb belongs to by looking at whether the last two letters of its infinitive form are *'ar', 'er' or 'ir'*. You will of course know them as *'ar', 'er' or 'ir' verbs.*

So, let's look at how regular verbs are formed in the present tense, starting with *'ar' verbs*.

Regular *'AR'* verb endings

To demonstrate, the regular verb *'hablar'* will be conjugated.

Hablar – To speak

I	*Yo*	*hablo*	(I speak)
You (sing.)	*Tú*	*hablas*	(You speak)
He/She/It	*Él/Ella*	*habla*	(He/She/It speaks)
We	*Nosotros/as*	*hablamos*	(We speak)
You (pl.)	*Vosotros/as*	*habláis*	(You speak)
They	*Ellos/Ellas*	*hablan*	(They speak)

Regular *'ER'* verb endings

To demonstrate, the regular verb *'vender'* will be conjugated.

Vender – To sell

I	*Yo*	*vendo*	(I sell)
You (sing.)	*Tú*	*vendes*	(You sell)

He/She/It	Él/Ella	vende	(He/She/It sells)
We	Nosotros/as	vendemos	(We sell)
You (pl.)	Vosotros/as	vendéis	(You sell)
They	Ellos/Ellas	venden	(They sell)

Regular 'IR' verb endings

To demonstrate, the regular verb 'vivir' will be conjugated.

Vivir – To live

I	Yo	vivo	(I live)
You (sing.)	Tú	vives	(You live)
He/She/It	Él/Ella	vive	(He/She/It lives)
We	Nosotros/as	vivimos	(We live)
You (pl.)	Vosotros/as	vivís	(You live)
They	Ellos/Ellas	viven	(They live)

The preterite tense

The Spanish preterite tense is used similarly to how it is in English, to talk about what has happened in the past, with simple sentences such as 'I went to the cinema.' The main difference is that when this same sentence is said in Spanish: 'Fui al cine', the subject of the sentence is revealed with the verb's conjugation, not through the use of pronouns such as 'I', 'you' or 'him/her', which are used much less frequently in Spanish than they are in English.

Again, except for several (and often common) irregular verbs, you will know how to conjugate a particular verb by seeing if it is an 'ar', 'er' or 'ir' verb.

So, let's look at how regular verbs are formed in the preterite tense, starting with 'ar' verbs.

Regular 'AR' verb endings

To demonstrate, the regular verb 'hablar' will be conjugated.

Hablar – To speak

I	**Yo**	habl**é**	(I spoke)
You (sing.)	**Tú**	habl**aste**	(You spoke)
He/She/It	**Él/Ella**	habl**ó**	(He/She/It spoke)
We	**Nosotros/as**	habl**amos**	(We spoke)
You (pl.)	**Vosotros/as**	habl**asteis**	(You spoke)
They	**Ellos/Ellas**	habl**aron**	(They spoke)

Regular 'ER' verb endings

To demonstrate, the regular verb 'vender' will be conjugated.

Vender – To sell

I	**Yo**	vend**í**	(I sold)
You (sing.)	**Tú**	vend**iste**	(You sold)
He/She/It	**Él/Ella**	vend**ió**	(He/She/It sold)
We	**Nosotros/as**	vend**imos**	(We sold)
You (pl.)	**Vosotros/as**	vend**isteis**	(You sold)
They	**Ellos/Ellas**	vend**ieron**	(They sold)

Regular 'IR' verb endings

To demonstrate, the regular verb 'vivir' will be conjugated.

Vivir – To live

	Yo	*vivi*	(I lived)
You (sing.)	**Tú**	*viviste*	(You lived)
He/She/It	**Él/Ella**	*vivió*	(He/She/It lived)
We	**Nosotros/as**	*vivimos*	(We lived)
You (pl.)	**Vosotros/as**	*vivisteis*	(You lived)
They	**Ellos/Ellas**	*vivieron*	(They lived)

The perfect tense

In Spanish, the perfect tense is used very similarly as it is in English – to explain what *has* happened in the past. It is constructed with 'to have' as the auxiliary verb, in conjunction with a past participle. For example, the phrase 'I have come back to the UK' is in the perfect tense, whereas the phrase 'I came back to the UK' is in the preterite tense.

It is a very similar story in Spanish, with the verb *'haber'* (to have) used as the infinitive in the perfect tense. For example: *'He vuelto al Reino Unido.'*

'He' is the auxiliary verb, and *'vuelto'* is the past participle.

As you can see, you do not need to worry about whether a verb is an *'ar'*, *'er'* or *'ir'* verb when using the perfect tense, just about the correct conjugation of the auxiliary verb (*haber*) for the subject you wish to discuss. The only other thing you need to know is the past participle of the verb which accompanies the subject, which never changes!

See below for an example phrase in the perfect tense, using each conjugation of *haber* with a selection of some common verbs' past participles:

I	**He**	*ido*	⟹	I have gone
You (sing.)	**Has**	*hecho*	⟹	You have done
He/She/It	**Ha**	*oído*	⟹	He/She/It has heard
We	**Hemos**	*visto*	⟹	We have seen
You (pl.)	**Habéis**	*dicho*	⟹	You have said
They	**Han**	*venido*	⟹	They have come

The imperfect tense

The imperfect tense is used very similarly in Spanish as it is in English; to refer to ongoing or incomplete events that happened in the past. The distinction between this tense and the perfect or preterite tense lies in whether the action has a clear start and end time, or if it was completed. If the action you wish to convey is not known or ambiguous, or is incomplete, use the imperfect tense

The main uses of the imperfect tense are:

- To describe past states and situations (e.g. During Dickens's time, only the most privileged children had access to education.)
- To describe what used to happen/recurring events that took place in the past (e.g. During my childhood, I played football every Sunday.)

So, let's look at how regular verbs are formed in the imperfect tense, starting with 'ar' verbs.

Regular 'AR' verb endings

To demonstrate, the regular verb 'hablar' will be conjugated.

Hablar – To speak

	Yo	hablaba	(I was speaking)
You (sing.)	Tú	hablabas	(You were speaking)
He/She/It	Él/Ella	hablaba	(He/She was speaking)
We	Nosotros/as	hablábamos	(We were speaking)
You (pl.)	Vosotros/as	hablabais	(You were speaking)
They	Ellos/Ellas	hablaban	(They were speaking)

Regular 'ER' verb endings

To demonstrate, the regular verb 'vender' will be conjugated.

Vender – To sell

I	Yo	vendía	(I was selling)
You (sing.)	Tú	vendías	(You were selling)
He/She/It	Él/Ella	vendía	(He/She was selling)
We	Nosotros/as	vendíamos	(We were selling)
You (pl.)	Vosotros/as	vendíais	(You were selling)
They	Ellos/Ellas	vendían	(They were selling)

Regular 'IR' verb endings

To demonstrate, the regular verb 'vivir' will be conjugated.

Vivir – To live

I	Yo	vivía	(I was living)
You (sing.)	Tú	vivías	(You were living)
He/She/It	Él/Ella	vivía	(He/She/It was living)

We	**Nosotros/as**	*vivíamos*	(We were living)
You (pl.)	**Vosotros/as**	*vivíais*	(You were living)
They	**Ellos/Ellas**	*vivían*	(They were living)

The future

As in English, the Spanish future tense modifies verbs in two ways – one for saying **what will happen** (the future tense), and one for saying **what is going to happen** (the immediate future).

The difference between the two languages appears when saying **what will happen**, as in Spanish verb endings are used to express this idea, rather than a word equivalent to 'will' in this instance.

But, the verb 'to go' ('*ir*') plus an infinitive is similarly used when saying **what is going to happen** in Spanish.

So, let's look at how regular verbs are formed in the future tenses, starting with the future tense.

The future tense

Regular '*AR*' verb endings

To demonstrate, the regular verb '*hablar*' will be conjugated.

Hablar – To speak

I	**Yo**	*hablaré*	(I will speak)
You (sing.)	**Tú**	*hablarás*	(You will speak)
He/She/It	**Él/Ella**	*hablará*	(He/She will speak)

We	**Nosotros/as**	*hablar***emos**	(We will speak)
You (pl.)	**Vosotros/as**	*hablar***éis**	(You will speak)
They	**Ellos/Ellas**	*hablar***án**	(They will speak)

Regular 'ER' verb endings

To demonstrate, the regular verb '*vender*' will be conjugated.

Vender – To sell

I	**Yo**	*vender***é**	(I will sell)
You (sing.)	**Tú**	*vender***ás**	(You will sell)
He/She/It	**Él/Ella**	*vender***á**	(He/She/It will sell)
We	**Nosotros/as**	*vender***emos**	(We will sell)
You (pl.)	**Vosotros/as**	*vender***eis**	(You will sell)
They	**Ellos/Ellas**	*vender***án**	(They will sell)

Regular 'IR' verb endings

To demonstrate, the regular verb '*vivir*' will be conjugated.

Vivir – To live

I	**Yo**	*vivir***é**	(I will live)
You (sing.)	**Tú**	*vivir***ás**	(You will live)
He/She/It	**Él/Ella**	*vivir***á**	(He/She/It will live)
We	**Nosotros/as**	*vivir***emos**	(We will live)
You (pl.)	**Vosotros/as**	*vivir***éis**	(You will live)
They	**Ellos/Ellas**	*vivir***án**	(They will live)

The immediate future

Regular *'AR'* verb endings

To demonstrate, the regular verb *'hablar'* will be conjugated.

Hablar – To speak

Yo	**voy**	*a*	*hablar*	(I am going to speak)
Tú	**vas**	*a*	*hablar*	(You are going to speak)
Él/Ella	**va**	*a*	*hablar*	(He/She is going to speak)
Nosotros/as	**vamos**	*a*	*hablar*	(We are going to speak)
Vosotros/as	**vais**	*a*	*hablar*	(You are going to speak)
Ellos/Ellas	**van**	*a*	*hablar*	(They are going to speak)

Regular *'ER'* verb endings

To demonstrate, the regular verb *'vender'* will be conjugated.

Vender – To sell

Yo	**voy**	*a*	*vender*	(I am going to sell)
Tú	**vas**	*a*	*vender*	(You are going to sell)
Él/Ella	**va**	*a*	*vender*	(He/She is going to sell)
Nosotros/as	**vamos**	*a*	*vender*	(We are going to sell)
Vosotros/as	**vais**	*a*	*vender*	(You are going to sell)
Ellos/Ellas	**van**	*a*	*vender*	(They are going to sell)

Regular '*IR*' verb endings

To demonstrate, the regular verb '*vivir*' will be conjugated.

Vivir – To live

Yo	**voy**	a	vivir	(I am going to live)
Tú	**vas**	a	vivir	(You are going to live)
Él/Ella	**va**	a	vivir	(He/She is going to live)
Nosotros/as	**vamos**	a	vivir	(We are going to live)
Vosotros/as	**vais**	a	vivir	(You are going to live)
Ellos/Ellas	**van**	a	vivir	(They are going to live)

The conditional tense

The conditional tense in Spanish is just as common as in English, and can be defined in a simple way as the tense that expresses what 'would happen'.

For example – 'If Man City signed Lionel Messi, **they would win** the Champions League.'

It can also be used when telling someone to do something, or when making a request.

For example – '**Could you** stop poking me on Facebook, please?' or '**I'd like** a glass of lemonade.'

So, let's look at how regular verbs are formed in the conditional tense in Spanish.

Regular 'AR' verb endings

To demonstrate, the regular verb 'hablar' will be conjugated.

Hablar – To speak

I	**Yo**	*hablaría*	(I would speak)
You (sing.)	**Tú**	*hablarías*	(You would speak)
He/She/It	**Él/Ella**	*hablaría*	(He/She would speak)
We	**Nosotros/as**	*hablaríamos*	(We would speak)
You (pl.)	**Vosotros/as**	*hablaríais*	(You would speak)
They	**Ellos/Ellas**	*hablarían*	(They would speak)

Regular 'ER' verb endings

To demonstrate, the regular verb 'vender' will be conjugated.

Vender – To sell

I	**Yo**	*vendería*	(I would sell)
You (sing.)	**Tú**	*venderías*	(You would sell)
He/She/It	**Él/Ella**	*vendería*	(He/She would sell)
We	**Nosotros/as**	*venderíamos*	(We would sell)
You (pl.)	**Vosotros/as**	*venderíais*	(You would sell)
They	**Ellos/Ellas**	*venderían*	(They would sell)

Regular '*IR*' verb endings

To demonstrate, the regular verb '*vivir*' will be conjugated.

Vivir – To live

	Yo	*viviría*	(I would live)
You (sing.)	**Tú**	*vivirías*	(You would live)
He/She/It	**Él/Ella**	*viviría*	(He/She/It would live)
We	**Nosotros/as**	*viviríamos*	(We would live)
You (pl.)	**Vosotros/as**	*viviríais*	(You would live)
They	**Ellos/Ellas**	*vivirían*	(They would live)

ANSWERS

My timetable

1. 9am
2. 1pm
3. 7:55am
4. Mo
5. Josie
6. Mo

Planning a party

1. A
2. C
3. C
4. B
5. B
6. A

My family life

1. She has no independence and her parents are too strict.
2. 3 – his father, his twin brother and his older sister.
3. 0 – He is the oldest child.
4. She was sad.
5. Because boys had been invited.
6. He is not always the centre of attention.
7. His mother needs the help – it's that simple.
8. As an intruder.

Daily routine

1. me despierto
2. me levanto
3. quedarme
4. me ducho

5. me cepillo
6. me visto
7. tomo
8. salir
9. llego
10. vuelvo
11. relajarme
12. ayudar
13. arreglar
14. hacer
15. preparar
16. me acuesto
17. me conecto
18. dormirme

Gorda Bretaña

1. The UK has the highest rates of obesity in Western Europe.
   OR
   24.9% of the British population is considered 'obese'.
   OR
   50% of the British population could be obese by 2050.

2. The sedentary nature of our lives.
   AND
   The omnipresence of health hazards in modern life.

3. We cannot continue down this harmful road (of unhealthiness).

4. **ANY TWO FROM:**
   o Take action against binge-drinking.
   o Raise taxes on tobacco.
   o Lower the costs of memberships to gyms/sports clubs.

5. Sleeping well

   AND

   Managing stress effectively

6. **WORDS TO THE EFFECT OF:**

   If we do not confront the serious problem of obesity in a decisive manner we will bring ourselves to disaster.

My hobbies

1. False – he uses music to switch off and relax.

2. True

3. Not mentioned

4. False – he thinks television is a waste of time.

5. True

6. False – he mentions having skated in the street before the construction o the skatepark.

7. True

8. True

The evolution of tourism

1. City breaks are as popular as beach holidays.

2. They are now abandoning their 'second homes' in Spain in order to explore new places.

3. The price of air travel is going down, and the number of destinations tha airlines serve is going up.

4. The revolution of smartphone culture.

5. More and more short breaks are being booked each spring, summer and autumn.

5. British people are becoming more adventurous with their choice of destination.

AND

The costs surrounding air travel are going down.

AND

The rise of the hyper-informed tourist.

Benefits and Risks of Social Media

Los beneficios

Plataformas como Facebook pueden sensibilizar al público sobre temas importantes.	You can instantly connect with friends to plan an event.
Tener un perfil de internet enseña a los jóvenes a desarrollar sus identidades, y a encontrar una voz propia y personal.	It's easy to share your life's best moments with your friends.
Se puede conectar instantáneamente con amigos para planear un evento.	Platforms like Facebook can raise public awareness about important subjects.
Es fácil compartir los mejores momentos de tu vida con tus amigos.	Social networks are great for keeping in touch with loved ones.
Las redes sociales son perfectas para mantenerse en contacto con los seres queridos.	Having an Internet profile teaches young people to develop their identities and find a distinct voice of their own.

Los riesgos

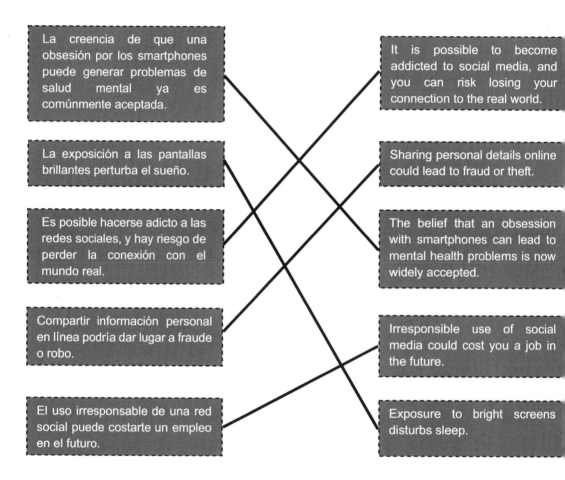

La creencia de que una obsesión por los smartphones puede generar problemas de salud mental ya es comúnmente aceptada.

La exposición a las pantallas brillantes perturba el sueño.

Es posible hacerse adicto a las redes sociales, y hay riesgo de perder la conexión con el mundo real.

Compartir información personal en línea podría dar lugar a fraude o robo.

El uso irresponsable de una red social puede costarte un empleo en el futuro.

It is possible to become addicted to social media, and you can risk losing your connection to the real world.

Sharing personal details online could lead to fraud or theft.

The belief that an obsession with smartphones can lead to mental health problems is now widely accepted.

Irresponsible use of social media could cost you a job in the future.

Exposure to bright screens disturbs sleep.

Charity

1. True
2. False – he believes the welfare system is 'effective'.
3. True
4. True
5. Not mentioned
6. False – he believes that homeless people need to 'make more of an effort to better themselves'.
7. Not mentioned
8. True

School life and the future

1. His marks have always been good.
2. She chose to prioritise music.
3. He has a complete lack of inspiration as to what he wants to do.
4. He expects to land a job at a high-level company.
5. She hopes to become the best musician the world has ever seen.
6. He does not want to think about the future.

DO YOU WISH TO STUDY ANOTHER FOREIGN LANGUAGE?

GCSE French is Easy: the ultimate guide for anyone who finds French challenging and for those wanting to pass GCSE French with ease. This exciting new guide is filled with fun and interesting facts for you to understand French in a way that makes it more compelling to learn, and more importantly, easier to understand! , and more importantly, easier to understand!

FOR MORE INFORMATION ON OUR GCSE FRENCH IS EASY GUIDE, PLEASE VISIT:

WWW.HOW2BECOME.COM